$12.95

J
599.74
Wo

Wolpert, Tom
Wolves

## DATE DUE

| | | |
|---|---|---|
| FE 24 '92 | AUG 28 '98 | JY 30 01 |
| MR 9'09 | NOV 28 '98 | JE 27 02 |
| MR 17'92 | MAR 27 '97 | AG 22 02 |
| AP 3'92 | AP 10 '97 | OC 12 02 |
| AP 11'92 | JUL 16 | JE 09 |
| OC 26'92 | NOV 19 | JA 05 '18 |
| NO 19'92 | DEC 08 '97 | |
| MY 7'9 | MAR 26 '98 | |
| MY 01 05 | N 24 '98 | |
| NOV 18 95 | DEC 17 '98 | |
| DEC 22 '98 | AP 09 '09 | |
| JUL 09 '98 | | |

DEMCO

*by Tom Wolpert*

# WOLVES

*Wolf Magic for Kids*

Gareth Stevens Children's Books

**MILWAUKEE**

**For a free color catalog describing Gareth Stevens' list of high-quality children's books, call 1-800-341-3569 (USA) or 1-800-461-9120 (Canada).**

**Library of Congress Cataloging-in-Publication Data**

Wolpert, Tom.
    Wolf magic for kids / by Tom Wolpert.
        p.   cm. — (Animal magic for kids)
    Includes index.
    Summary: An introduction to the physical characteristics, behavior, habitat,
and ability to communicate of the wolf.
    ISBN 0-8368-0662-X
    1. Wolves—Juvenile literature. [1. Wolves.] I. Title. II. Series.
QL737.C22W646     1991
599.74'442—dc20                           90-50720

This North American edition published by
**Gareth Stevens Children's Books**
1555 North RiverCenter Drive, Suite 201
Milwaukee, Wisconsin 53212, USA

First published in 1990 by NorthWord Press, Inc., with a text by Tom Wolpert.
Copyright © 1990 by NorthWord Press, Inc.

Printed in the United States of America

1 2 3 4 5 6 7 8 9 97 96 95 94 93 92 91

The wolf is an animal we have heard about in fables and fairy tales. Because of those tales, we sometimes think that the wolf is a ferocious animal that attacks and eats humans. But this is not true. In fact, the wolf is the *ancestor* of our oldest animal friend - the dog.

Almost all wolves in North America belong to a species called the gray wolf. A wolf looks like a large, shaggy version of a German Shepard. But, a wolf has longer legs and larger feet. A wolf's head is larger and more rounded. His eyes are set further apart. The cheeks of a wolf bulge with jaw muscles.

Male wolves are usually two and a half to three feet tall and weigh seventy-five to one hundred pounds. The largest wolf ever found weighed 175 pounds. Wolves this large are rare. Female wolves are smaller than males. They are usually one and a half to two and a half feet tall. A female wolf weighs sixty to eighty pounds. Wolves in Canada and Alaska are larger than wolves in the southern United States.

Wolves are found in many colors. Their color depends on their *environment*. Wolves are most often colored gray. However, some may be brown, golden brown, rusty red or almost any combination of these colors. Some are all black and others pure white. The arctic wolf is pure white.

The belly and throat of the wolf is usually light in color and almost white. The wolf's legs, ears and nose are often light brown. The face and back are usually marked with dark brown or black.

The timber wolf is often called the "gray wolf" because of its thick gray fur. The wolves of central Canada are usually gray. Wolves that live in the treeless plains of northern arctic regions and forests of Canada and Alaska may also be gray. Because of this, scientists have nicknamed all wolves that live in North America the gray wolf.

There are many wolves that live in the forests of Alaska, Canada, and northern Minnesota. A few wolves also live in upper Michigan and northern Wisconsin. These wolves are called "timber wolves" because they live among the trees. Most timber wolves are dark gray or black. Their home in the forest is shadowy and dark. The wolves' dark coats provide excellent *camouflage*.

Wolves that live in northern Alaska and Canada are called "tundra wolves." They live on the treeless plains or tundra. Tundra wolves are the most beautiful wolves in North America. They have beautiful thick fur to protect them from the cold. Some of these wolves are pure white so they can hide easily in the snow.

A few wolves still live in Arizona, Arkansas, Mississippi, Missouri, New Mexico and North Dakota. These wolves are smaller than those that live in the far north. They are gray in color.

The red wolf is a different species from the gray wolf. The red wolf lives in wilderness areas of Texas and Louisiana. The red wolf is nearly *extinct*.

Today in the United States, the gray wolf remains in large numbers only in Alaska and northern Minnesota. Between 5,000 and 15,000 gray wolves live in Alaska. About 1,200 live in northern Minnesota.

In late winter, the lakes are frozen and snow still covers the ground. Female wolves are able to become pregnant for only a few days during this time. During her first mating season, a young female will choose a mate that will be her partner for life. If one of the couple should die, the other one usually will never mate again.

The pregnant female begins digging a den three to four weeks before her pups arrive. She often searches several days to find the right spot. Her den must be on high ground so water does not seep into it. She may also choose a rock cave or even a hollow log for her den. However, the den must be near a river or a stream. This is important. Once the female starts to nurse her young, she will need to drink a lot of water.

Wolf dens are quite large. The front entrance is large enough for a person to crawl through. A tunnel leads from the entrance to the chamber where the pups are kept. The tunnel may be six to fourteen feet long. The chamber is large enough for the mother to stand. Sometimes there are two chambers, one for the pups and one for the mother to rest.

Sixty to sixty-two days after the parent wolves mate, the pups are born. Newborn wolves are called pups. While waiting for the pups to be born, the entire wolf family to which the parent wolves belong stays close to the den. This family, or pack, hunts for food close by the den instead of going on long hunts.

The day before the pups arrive, the female goes inside the den and stays until the pups are born. Her mate stands guard outside the entrance.

The newborn pups are now members of the pack. Packs are family groups. Every wolf is born into a pack. The most basic pack will include a father, mother and a litter of pups. The leader of the pack is almost always a male. This leader will decide when the pack can go on a hunt and when the pack can rest. All other wolves in the pack obey the leader.

When a pack makes a kill, the wolves wait and let the leader have the first choice of meat. Once the leader starts eating, the others join and begin to feed, too.

When the wolves have finished feeding, they move on to the leader's resting spot of choice. After resting, the leader walks up to the other members of the pack and wakes them.

There is also a female leader of the pack. She is in charge of all the other females in the pack. Sometimes she helps the male leader make the other wolves obey his commands. The male leader is usually the chief wolf in the whole pack. However, when the male and female leaders have pups, the female becomes the head wolf. She remains the head wolf

until her pups are old enough to travel and hunt with the pack. Then the father wolf becomes the head wolf once again.

Some wolf packs have as many as thirty-six members. In these large packs there are many adults. However, there is still only one male and female leader.

About two weeks after they are born, the pups are able to open their eyes. They learn to stand and then to walk. Their front teeth come in at this time. Now they begin chewing on each other's tails. By the time they are three weeks old, they can hear and see very well. Now it is time for them to go outside the den for the first time.

The other pack members become very excited when they see the pups for the first time. The pack members wag their tails and gather around the pups and lick them. This is the first time the father is able to get close to his pups.

All the wolves are very protective of pups in the pack. During the next several months, the pups spend a lot of time playing outside the den. Many pack members will take turns standing guard over the pups. If the mother must leave to get food, another adult will "baby-sit" the pups for her.

When the pups are about four weeks old, they begin to eat solid food. When an adult wolf returns from eating a meal, the pups swarm around it. The adult then ejects the food in its stomach in front of the hungry pups. The pups then eat this food that was brought to them in the stomach of the adult wolf.

Carrying the meat back in their stomachs has advantages for the adult wolves. If the wolf carried the meat back in its mouth, the food would get covered with dust, sand and dirt. Also the smell of the meat would leave a scent trail for other animals to follow to the den. A bear, wolverine, fisher or lynx could follow the trail and kill the young pups. So when the adult wolves bring the meat back in their stomachs, the meat arrives fresh, warm, undigested, and clean. Also, the location of the den remains a secret from other animals.

The pups begin to learn the ways of adult wolves when they are about three months of age. Then the mother no longer allows the pups to sleep in the den. The pups begin to sleep outside with the rest of the wolves. When the pups begin to sleep outside, the other wolves in the pack begin to go on longer hunts. Several of the younger adult wolves stay behind with the pups. After several days, the pack returns to the den area and the waiting pups.

Wolves are master hunters. Wolves eat very large animals or many small animals, depending on what type of *prey* is available. Wolves kill sick or injured caribou, moose or deer that would be a burden to the rest of their herd. The wolves will travel miles in search of food for themselves and their

young pups. The timber wolf often travels along the tops of ridges when hunting. From the tops of these ridges the wolves can look down for prey. When the prey is spotted, the wolves rush down to capture it.

The wolf is a powerful runner. It can run for long distances. However, it cannot run at very high speeds. A wolf can outrun a human, but has trouble overtaking hoofed animals. Wolves solve this problem by hunting in packs. Hunting in packs allows the wolves to circle their prey. The prey is then caught in the middle and cannot run from the wolves.

A wolf can survive for two weeks without eating. During this time it will hunt and chase many animals. Finally, it will find one it can kill.

Wolves journey far and wide while hunting. The pack usually travels about five miles an hour, in a single file. In search of food, the wolves travel on frozen waterways, windswept ridges, and old roads and trails.

The pack may have to travel many miles in a day to find a herd of animals to prey upon. Wolves always travel at a steady trot and rarely walk. Wolves can travel forty miles without rest.

Wolves track down prey animals by using their keen sense of smell. As the pack gets closer to the herd of prey animals, the smell of the prey gets stronger. Wolves do not rush in at the herd. They stay back and study it. The pack looks for an animal that is old, sick or very young. These animals cannot run as fast. The pack knows these animals are easier to catch.

Wolves actually help keep herds of deer and other animals healthy. Killing the old or sick members of a herd leaves more food for the other herd members. With more food, the healthy animals are able to have strong, healthy young.

Once wolves make a kill, they can eat a large amount. The expression - "to eat like a wolf" - comes from their eating habits. A healthy adult wolf can eat twenty pounds of meat at one feeding.

When members of the pack have finished eating the meat, they wander off to a sunny place to rest. After sleeping for several hours, they return to their kill. After eating any meat that is left, they spend hours chewing on the bones. This keeps their teeth clean and strong, and supplies them with necessary minerals.

Wolves are very good communicators. They use sounds and gestures to "show talk" to other members in their pack. Wolves can make a variety of sounds. Each sound has its own meaning. If a wolf is restless or excited, it whimpers. Wolves also whimper when they bring food to the pups.

A snarl means that a wolf is threatening another wolf. It is a warning. It is a way of telling other wolves that they are making the snarling wolf unhappy.

A short "wuff" is a warning sound. When a member of the pack senses danger, it makes a "wuff" sound. If the danger becomes stronger, the "wuff" turns into a bark. When pack members hear a bark, they know it is time to flee.

The wolf is probably best known for its howling. A wolf howling alone produces a low, mournful cry. When several wolves howl together, their voices blend together. Some wolves also yip and some yowl. Others moan, whine, bark or wail.

Scientists are not sure why wolves howl. Some people say wolves howl because they are lonely. Others say wolves howl to find other wolves. However, most scientists think that wolf packs howl to tell other wolf packs to stay away from their territory. This howling also helps to bond the pack together.

Only in recent years have we begun to understand the wolf. Wolves are interesting and beautiful animals. Ordinarily, wolves are afraid of people and will flee when encountered by them. Not one case of healthy wolves attacking people has been recorded in North America.

As we learn more about our environment, it becomes clear that the wolf is an essential part of nature. Where the wolf lives, it helps keep prey animals from becoming so *abundant* that they starve or die of disease. When the prey animals are not abundant, the wolves do not have pups. That way, the number of wolves stays low and members of the wolf pack do not have to share with pups what little meat they can catch.

Wolves must kill other animals in order to live. But like eagles, foxes, bears, and other *predators* that also eat animals, the wolf and its prey have survived and lived together in the same places for many thousands of years.

## GLOSSARY

The words below also appear in the text in *italicized* type. The page number on which each word first appears is listed after each definition.

*Abundant:* In plentiful supply (page 47).

*Ancestor:* A relative from long ago (page 5).

*Camouflage:* A way to hide by blending in with the surrounding area (page 11).

*Environment:* The surroundings of an animal, including the landscape, weather, and food conditions (page 9).

*Extinct:* No longer in existence as a species (page 13).

*Predators:* Animals that live by eating other animals (page 47).

*Prey:* A creature hunted or caught for food (page 34).

## ADULT-CHILD INTERACTION QUESTIONS

*These are questions you may ask young readers to get them to think about wolves as viable occupants of a niche in the food chain. Encourage them to explain their feelings about wolves and to ask their own questions. Clarify any misunderstandings they may have about the predator-prey relationship as it relates to wolves, and explain the need to have both predators and prey in the world. In this way, you can help foster future generations of environmentally aware and appreciative adults.*

1. Why do you think wolves need coats that provide good camouflage?

2. How are wolf pups and human babies alike?

3. Why do you think the mother wolf no longer allows the pups to sleep in the den after they are three months old?

4. Why do you think people have made up scary stories about wolves? Do you think wolves are bad? Why?

5. Would you like to belong to a wolf pack? Why?